ANOTHER PHASE

ANOTHER PHASE

ॐ

poems

Eloise Klein Healy

🐓 Red Hen Press | *Pasadena, CA*

Book layout by Amber Lucido

Library of Congress Cataloging-in-Publication Data
Names: Healy, Eloise Klein, author.
Title: Another phase : poems / Eloise Klein Healy.
Description: First edition. | Pasadena, CA : Red Hen Press, [2018]
Identifiers: LCCN 2018031077 | ISBN 9781597090421 (tradepaper)
Classification: LCC PS3558.E234 A6 2018 | DDC 811/.54—dc23
LC record available at https://lccn.loc.gov/2018031077

The National Endowment for the Arts, the Los Angeles County Arts Commission, the Ahmanson Foundation, the Dwight Stuart Youth Fund, the Max Factor Family Foundation, the Pasadena Tournament of Roses Foundation, the Pasadena Arts & Culture Commission and the City of Pasadena Cultural Affairs Division, the City of Los Angeles Department of Cultural Affairs, the Audrey & Sydney Irmas Charitable Foundation, the Kinder Morgan Foundation, the Meta & George Rosenberg Foundation, the Allergan Foundation, the Riordan Foundation, and the Amazon Literary Partnership partially support Red Hen Press.

First Edition
Published by Red Hen Press
www.redhen.org

For Betty

Contents

Imagine this:

You cannot understand what you hear or read. You cannot speak or write and be understood. Your use of language has been lost. You speak and write words in a nonsensical manner. You hear what people say, but it makes no sense.

In 2013, this happened to Eloise Klein Healy, who had recently been named the first Poet Laureate of Los Angeles.

The day before her illness she was participating with Caroline Kennedy Schlosberg in an interview and reading at the ALOUD series at the Downtown Los Angeles Library. The next day she was hospitalized with viral encephalitis resulting in a diagnosis of encephalopathy with severe Wernicke's Aphasia. The result was the loss of ability to use language. It's rare that there is functional language recovery. In Eloise's case, her language returned with exceptional poetic ability.

Recovery has been a long, intense process. Eloise has weekly speech-language therapy and a village of family and friends to help with daily intense practice of all language modalities. The recovery of her poetic abilities has been a unique, previously undocumented neuroscience phenomenon.

It has been a rare privilege to help guide Eloise through an uncharted therapeutic process toward newness and novelty in her unique language creations. BRAVO!

Betty L. McMicken, Ph.D.
Speech-Language Pathologist
Clinical Professor, Chapman University
Associate Professor Emeritus, CSU Long Beach
Assistant Clinical Professor, UC Irvine Medical Center

ANOTHER PHASE

ONCE UPON A TIME

Five o'clock in the morning,
I wake up. A call, a window,
the sky is barely alert.
Every day the stars see it all,
but I know about loving first.

TO

What to do today?
To drive along, a tune
to play. To choose two
songs again, to swing again.
Too happy? No way!

OHHH

Take a DEEP breath.
Today is over,
lots of names, places,
and how I listen.
What I don't say—thank you.

ARTEMIS

Sweet time with friends, discussing life,
honor, arts. I remember, too,
the ark we've talked about, deep
water, days. A start. Then, Nikita
barking. Remember Arktoi Books, our famous friends.

WONDER

Full of wonder? Ouch!
Wonder what it means
to be full of feelings. What about
how I know, how I ask
about pain? But sorrow? Tell.

ANOTHER PHASE

It's hard for me to read the LA Times.
I want to relearn, to reline part of me.
How did my brain twist?
How did the whack of it phase me?
Every page. Every word blank.

EVERYWHERE

how haiku chimes
the old bell heavy
on the rhymes a wind comes
and sings it too
any day any air haiku everywhere

DANCING

Dancing in the living room,
we're swinging and swaying,
laughing with all the lines.
I "know fascination" and another
does a fox trot. Two nearly girls, boppin'.

UP

Another day, but am I duller?
Nothing done and not a dollar
bill for every hour. Happiness
will help if hope could find
my mind and smooth it all.

PROBLEM

When first I wrote a poem,
I couldn't change anything.
Didn't plan to edit or write another.
"Brain-fry" was my reality time.
Step two wasn't there yet.

SWING

I woke up and found the swing
when I lived right by my church.
There were three or four playgrounds
at St. Mary's which I learned
to pump, fly high, and let go, higher yet.

DISCUSS

I know how to talk and you hear me.
But discuss it again about what I mean,
what I have lost. Try it again anyway.
Forget the pain, discuss with me or restrain
but I know, I know about my heart.

AWAKE

At 3:00 a.m., I open my eyes.
No reason. No barking dogs next door.
But in the middle of the night,
here come the words.
Me listed by those already dead.

MUSIC?

I am a liar.
Mmm, maybe I'm a lyre. Music?
Truth or true
or wisdom or wrong?
Come on! Dumb?

FUR

"Vat's it fur?" he said.
"What's it for?" I thought.
Why I care is where I am,
but did I remember
the wild animal, that black bear?

ATTITUDE

I know about the word "information."
Now I've learned I "broke" my mind.
My words smeared me—aphasia.
My speaking could not count names or rhyme,
The "I/me/much" of mine. Gone. Lost.

KITE

Afternoon almost over
I'm already tired.
The kite is still flying
all over the place and the kiddo
hangs on with his hands. Hands on to sing.

IMAGINATION

It's imaging the nation, I know.
The whole bad-ass things bashing a broken trumpet.
Is this only a room you're now upholding
for your "presidential" affairs or are you invading?
Put it simply, I am still envisioning a better world.

TIPS

Oh, the fingertips that touch!
But this means less than possible.
Your body parts don't behave or feel like you've been on TV
or smooch my lips like dry blood.
I want to run fingers perfectly through your hair.

YZ?

A brain-clear, dear—engaging,
fierce. Good help if just keep living,
meeting—now over pain.
Quite reasonable. So true, using
verse, wisdom, X-tasy, your zone.

FLASHLIGHT

When did the flashlight get its name?
Didn't have one yet? That time was 2013.
I have a new word exactly now.
Not only the thing I hadn't said for three years.
Now, saying and using the flashlight. Big deal for sure!

WHOO . . .

"I'll take a nap," I say.
 She says, "Have an apple."
 What does she want?
 Give or take? Don't pay
 attention. Oh, oh—pissed at me.

LISTS

More than anything,
I keep failing.
The problem? Making
up my goal to do
what I'm hoping to, but I don't.

WOW

Turn it over and see
my penny. Such a bright one,
2016 still brand new.
Reminds me when I was born.
The old silver coin, 1943, and me.

PLACES

Most early nights, before I fall asleep
I say, "good bye," but mean, "I love you."
My breath lifts and falls and my memory
is as far away as it finds me. Every night
I slow down and soon have gone away.

ALL THE SPECIAL

Most of my special feelings
were about what my eyes meant.
But now my cataracts are gone.
My new eyes don't bother me much.
I keep seeing what I used to see. I see it all.

ANALYZING

Blank spots in the brain
try again and again to name
what one had said before,
handed from a new beginning,
waiting for the ground, the head, to meet.

BOTHERSOME WOMAN

How the older woman at Zoom Room
tried to keep "beating" me up.
What a loud mouth and bad ears!
I told her to shut up,
I have aphasia and I've had enough.

SKY

Here we doubt the pain,
the dead, the ground.
Bear it up, tear it down,
being done over or inside out.
Then, sky and blue-white moon.

PORCUPINE

My brain-word sounded like a porcupine or maybe "porque?"
How did I play between two words anyway?
It's almost how great regular words "pop."
That's what's really like a tune. A swing-a day, a sway.
These two songs in my head anyway.

DUMP

Dump truck is just driving by
but "Trump-luck!" or "Fuck Trump!"
calls up his lies and he's a fool/fouler,
a moody mouth-mauler.
So he's driven now! Driven?

PRIZE

"Ho hum" is just a word
  but what the body knows
  is written down and language
  is the prize. But what more could you want?
  Surprise yourself and never surmise.

MOON

Maybe I'm not awake.
I haven't looked outside yet
but now it's what to know.
The moon is still quiet,
not dark.

KNOTS

After the party, I've kissed everybody good night
though I probably don't remember all of them anymore.
Untying the laces from my knots is
all it takes. Breathing five deep breaths
and I'm leading my wacky body to my bed.

MEADOWLARK

Grinning—more than happy,
and not just smiling in the dark.
But I know a meadowlark's singing,
hearing low in the dark. I miss a poet
who lived here and had been dying, too.

READ

I used to read
faster than I read now.
I used my thoughts
and let them go.
Now, before I read, I sing.

LONG

Two girls with hands on all
and we use both
waists wrists
body mind
so so long

ANIMALS

All we are weighing
is give sheep a chance.
The day I am saying
is "water the plants."
And huff-a-low buffalo is here to the dance.

BORN

Born in El Paso, Texas
driven down to South Dakota.
Later, Ray & Carmen moved to Sioux City,
then Remsen, Iowa, and we first lived
a mile from town. I've loved first & first & first . . .

GOING FOR WORDS

Pencil, Pen, Power, Patience.
Can I begin plan, or plain, or please?
There's no beginning or end. Anything now.
New, Native, Nonchalant. Nervous.
I know more about me now. Aphasia.

ALPHABET

You know how you've drifted from
the wild tone of words—maybe alpha or beta.
Always choosing between A and B
the best chance is a bet.
It's win or lose but holding tightly.

FOOD

Spelt or not, I learned my truth!
Food wasn't just wheat, rye, or sour bread.
What was wrecking me saved me otherwise
when I got Whole Food around me
and my favorite brain—Ancient Grain!

WEATHER

What's it doing today?
Never more than three weeks
of rain here, but then sun—
hot, long, blue. Whether or not,
sad clouds can stay for days.

ASSHOLE

As wild as you could be,
you drank a ton per day.
Today you climbed your uphill steps
and crossed your street, just weaving.
Ended up as just an asshole. Maybe less.

HERE'S WHAT I SAID

My brain needs me
to knock out the haziness.
But don't cut the brain out.
Work on it. Just keep working.
Each day.

JOAN

In France, the woman died
long ago. Death by fire
and the loss of all her strength.
Not just this hero, one of a time only,
but how many burned inside or out?

MISS DANCING IN THE DARK

Oh, Miss Dancing In The Dark, when did you
choose me? Perhaps the days before I found
myself, let alone all the sweethearts
I kept losing. Yes, I wanted to believe I'd kiss
and find the heart I've been losing.

MY BRAIN, MY LOSS

Piles on my desk top, paper
after paper after paper.
What I wrote, rewrote, never tore.
Maybe one I tore and balled up.
Still writing poems. Try again. Loss.

MAPS

I love the maps so much I'm singing
my wacky "three-dee!" tunes and already
I need to stop and unfold them,
smooth them. Then this feeling emerges,
dimensional and wildly as free as Antarctica.

DAD

A mile out of town, Ray taught me
how to tie my shoe. Showing me
my left-handedness was really part of me.
"Good job!" he said, then went back to work,
one mile from Remsen, Iowa.

BUZZ

Dropped a little dope
to drive from LA to CSUN.
Also sang along, up and over,
knew I was stoned already,
flying high and danger buzzed me better.

DON'T

Don't miss, don't mess,
don't walk, don't talk.
It's pretty clear what you're all about.
But it's painful to say
I doubt you don't mean anything anyway.

EVER

Sometimes when I'm ill,
my head is a mirage.
Can I get better? Ever?
Can anything change it? But the brain
manages me. Rules it. Pain.

JUST

Just a little bit
of "lust." Just a better
word for "trust."
Better yet is to adjust
the name for "burst" first.

VISITOR

A new visit this morning.
Backyard covered with rain.
Yesterday & today & forever.
Quan Yin—she found me
in the black stone shape of her hands.

NOW

Wind, flying down screaming
whether you hear it or not.
You're awake now. The rain wracks
and blows and takes the windows.
California so quickly.

DECIDED

Though I've done this before,
I can't determine who
authorized my work.
I've never chosen to care
about any moment of their concerns.

SHOWS

for Betty McMicken

Bet she didn't like you,
but now it shows.
Attention isn't where anyone thinks, "ready."
A tension is what we know,
that it has already "showed."

AGAIN

Grumpy. Closes the door.
Then drops her blouse, clothes, iPhone.
What the hell is she doing?
Next, kicking her shoes across the hall.
That's it for her usually. Still nuts.

ALWAYS

I think of my life
but I've never been lazy.
Helping and talking, I've worked
so much my friends think I'm crazy.
OK, I'm tired enough, a little bit hazy.

THEIR WORLD

for Marie & Robi

More about the best.
You bet. Not a simple word
or wit or, well, wisdom.
No. It's more about love.
Not lingering. But living again. Again.

MONEY

Losers, keepers, but
all the savings
wreck the weepers,
tell a lie that causes
creepers, tell a secret, or cheat.

SKUNKS

Oh-ow-ooo! I thought I smelled
a skunk. But how could I see these kits
in New Mexico though I know exactly
when and there? Two baby ones.
Black and white rolling everywhere.

MIST

Last week before the rain
was ready to arrive, even the sky
seemed as far away as any of the clouds.
Above and below, the mist
floats aware and never ever missed.

AT LEAST OR AT LAST

How long I've worn a bra.
Certainly didn't come to remind me
about what my mom said, "OK, you need
to wear a bra." Not about the bra anymore.
Just the size of my mind that can doubt me.

TRAVEL

We drove to Morro Bay,
my town a long time ago.
The famous words, both
tears and joy were
"lost and found" again.

MIND

Had you changed your mind
or lost it? I'm more confused now
since I'd newly been like this.
My little brain flipped a coin and off I went.
Mindless, but not just for my time.

FIVE O'CLOCK

Bunching up. It's five o'clock and I'm feeling
the wacky but normal job of the day.
Eating all the pup's fine part,
and then our best time. Walking and sunlight
fading and everything gathers. Slows.

BODY

Not just a brain
or my mind. Body.
And how time begins
to swell, and then inside
all change and everyone. Oh, wild.

BIOGRAPHICAL NOTE

Eloise Klein Healy, the author of eight books of poetry including *A Wild Surmise*, was appointed the first poet laureate of the City of Los Angeles in 2012. Awarded the Publishing Triangle Lifetime Achievement Award in 2015, she also had artist residencies at the MacDowell Colony and Dorland Mountain Colony. She has received grants from the California Arts Council, the CSU Northridge Merit Award Program, and a COLA Fellowship from the City of Los Angeles. She directed the Women's Studies program at CSUN and taught in the Feminist Studio Workshop at The Woman's Building in Los Angeles. She was the founding chair of the MFA in Creative Writing program at Antioch University Los Angeles. Her imprint with Red Hen Press, Arktoi Books, specializes in publishing high-quality literary work by lesbian authors.